9-11

Meditations at the Center of the World

9-11

Meditations at the Center of the World

Eugene Kennedy

ORBIS BOOKS

Maryknoll, New York 10545

Second Printing, September 2002

Photo Credits:
Gudrun Mertes-Frady / *Here Is New York:* p. 16
Ricky Flores / *The Journal News:* p. 100
Seth Harrison / *The Journal News:* p. 25
Niko and Gina Plaitakis / *Here Is New York:* pp. 30, 44, 49, 54, 68, 73, 83
Joe Larese / *The Journal News:* p. 39
Stephen Schmitt / *The Journal News:* p. 59
Jay Manis/Manis Photo: p. 105

Founded in 1970, Orbis Books endeavors to publish works that enlighten the mind, nourish the spirit, and challenge the conscience. The publishing arm of the Maryknoll Fathers and Brothers, Orbis seeks to explore the global dimensions of the Christian faith and mission, to invite dialogue with diverse cultures and religious traditions, and to serve the cause of reconciliation and peace. The books published reflect the views of their authors and do not represent the official position of the Maryknoll Society. To learn more about Maryknoll and Orbis Books, please visit our website at www.maryknoll.org.

The meditations contained in this book are based on columns written for the Religion News Service, beginning with that of September 11, 2001, and continuing every week through the fall and early winter.

Published by Orbis Books, Maryknoll, NY 10545-0308

Manufactured in the United States of America

Library of Congress Cataloging-in-Publication Data

Kennedy, Eugene
    9-11 : meditations at the center of the world / Eugene Kennedy.
      p. cm.
    ISBN 1-57075-445-4 (pbk.)
    1. September 11 Terrorist Attacks, 2001. 2. Suffering—Religious aspects—Catholic Church—Meditations.   I. Title.
    BT732.7 .K46 2002
    242'.4—dc21

                                     2002007053

To

Rudolph Giuliani,
who mourned the dead
and led the living

Chief Black Elk spoke of
South Dakota's Harney Peak as

the earth mountain, the center of the world....
This vast tipi seemed to be as large
as the world itself....
The peoples that were there in that lodge,
they talked to me....

— Stephen Larsen,
The Mythic Imagination

Contents

Foreword   11

The Last Day of Ordinary Time   15

Maybe *This* Is the Greatest Generation   20

Listen to the Voices of the Ruins   24

What Judgment Day Is Really Like   29

Neutron Jack and the Jesuit   34

Saint Luke's Tooth and the Trade Towers   38

What Makes Anything Sacred?   43

All Saints Day/All Souls Day   48

Let the Living Bury Their Dead   53

The Site   58

Contents

Revelations at Thanksgiving   63

The Mountains at the Center of the World   67

Happy the Sorrowing for They Have
Known Love   72

Closing In on the Caves   77

The Christmas Mystery of the World As It Is   82

Cardinal Mahony, Mayor Giuliani,
and the Numbers Game   87

The Pain inside Pain   91

Lost/Found/Learned   95

The Eyes of 9/11   99

Build Anything, Ground Zero's Spirit
Will Still Be There   104

Notes   109

Foreword

The soul can split the sky in two,
And let the face of God shine through.
　　　　　　— Edna St. Vincent Millay

No one talked about what had truly sent us reeling.
It was not only the planes, the first one moving without hesitation toward the gleaming wall of the tower,
the second like a bad-dream ghost of the first, the
two skyscrapers collapsing gracefully amid a dove-
gray blizzard of debris. It was not only the tumult
after, the fighter planes crisscrossing the paralyzed
grid of Manhattan, the passersby frozen with their
faces turned up to the terrifying cloudless sky, the
smell of burnt everything hanging over it all.

It was not just the people, the fathers and mothers, the sons and daughters, the men and women, the
lawyers and bankers, the secretaries and waiters, the
cops and firefighters, the ones who fell from above and

the others who were crushed on the sidewalk where they stood.

It was that we felt it all in a place deep inside that some of us had ignored, some overlooked, some let lie fallow, some denied.

The twin towers were destroyed and the Pentagon damaged by planes that had been turned into bombs, by men who had been turned into murderers. It was the greatest cataclysm in any of our memories, the greatest act of terrorist aggression on American soil in this country's history. It happened in lower Manhattan and just outside of Washington, D.C.

And it happened in our souls, too.

It was why there was a kind of overweening empathy as persistent and powerful and unmistakable as the smell of smoke. It was how millions of strangers managed to reach out in their hearts to thousands of unknown victims and to their families, too. It was why even those nominally untouched by the events, a continent away, were shaken deep inside and began to think deeply, persistently, of what it means to be human and how precious is the casually handled gift of life.

The events of September 11 marked an unprecedented foreign policy crisis for the United States and its people. But it was also a great spiritual crisis, in which men and women who had perhaps been too otherwise engaged for soul searching found themselves blown by the explosion into the center of their own personal universe, forced into a face-to-face confrontation with mortality and meaning, the notion of God and the paradox of human existence, bounded on one side by great selflessness and on the other by mass destruction.

This was Eugene Kennedy's beat as a columnist who has spent much of his life reporting on the human soul. The rubble of the twin towers became, for this psychologist and former priest, a ground zero for the spirit. Never before in his long career of limning the world within us in prose had he had such an opportunity to understand what we are made of as when he looked upon the wreckage and saw the paradoxes of good and evil, destruction and resurrection.

Whether describing the sacramental search for the remains of those lost or the consecration of the site by the deaths of its martyrs and the work of its caretakers, Kennedy goes where our own hearts have led us since we first saw the pictures and heard the stories:

to that place inside ourselves where anguish lodges and teaches us to treasure our own blessings.

He calls these meditations, and they are his own thoughts, part of a great tradition of bringing private communion to bear upon public events. But we recognize in them our own thoughts and feelings, the inchoate unexpected that this great tragedy woke in us and that changed the emotional landscape of our lives as surely as the landscape of one city and all the nation was changed. We recognize, too, the changing landmarks of the months afterward, the movement of so many of our hearts from disbelief and anger to confusion and finally to understanding.

Amid the spars of metal, the firefighters' gray faces, the families armed with leaflets, the airline manifests, the precious detritus of daily life, we recognized our maybe lives. In Kennedy's words we recognize our certain souls, struggling toward peace amid tumult and a sky split open one day in September.

ANNA QUINDLEN

The Last Day of Ordinary Time

September 11, 2001. New York, New York. "The date," the ordinary looking lady said like a seer, "is 911." An emergency for all of us, this September day in 2001 that, like a September day in 1939, ended a dream of peace.

The headlines in that Tuesday's morning papers are the last picture we have of a world unaware that it would never be the same again. What people were excited about — who would be the next mayor of New York, political deals to revive the economy, whether Barry Bonds would break the home run record or Michael Jordan would play basketball again — were made suddenly trivial by Death's striking down thousands and searing all of us with twin lightning bolts of terrorism.

That morning promised a day of ravishing beauty, better even than the day before, that final ordinary

day when the leaves whispered of autumn but the thermometer sang still of summer and a brief electrical storm washed down Manhattan's dusty streets the way loosed hydrants do for playing children on the hottest days.

The sky was clear and the buildings stood fine edged against the glistening Atlantic waters, promises, each of these, of the coming glory of autumn in New York. One could look, as my wife and I did the evening before, at the Trade Towers in the last sunset that would ever gild their walls and sense that the fall had made its move against summer and change was in the air.

The clarity of the atmosphere only sharpened the razor strikes of the planes that slit the towers open like a man's wrists to lay blood sacrifice on the altar of lower Manhattan. And there rose a pillar of cloud by day that would not, as it did in the Old Testament, lead us safely out of the desert but more deeply into one than we have ever known before.

The ashes fell on all of us as we and our world were changed. For what we could feel was the edge of evil itself, evil not spread out in disguise by the devil, but evil brewed in the dark apothecary of the human heart, evil unleashed in its raw and indifferent power on the innocent, evil that did not come from another world but from our own.

This mystery seems as dark and impenetrable as the clouds of debris that brimmed above the lower buildings, rolled along the city streets, and finally totally engulfed the life we had shared until that moment.

What was altered on Tuesday morning was the ordinary, the everyday, life in its own seasons, complicated enough but sweetly simple compared to life under the shadow of dread, that feeling that, for reasons unconnected with them and perhaps by now beyond being understood by anyone, good men and women could no longer be sure of that ordinary life, could no longer be sure that ordinary time, as it is called in the Catholic liturgy, would ever exist again.

For most of us, ordinary time is all that we have. It is our chance for simple glory, for waking to the wonders of the world and of each other, for making friends and falling in love, and giving and encouraging life in a generation beyond us.

Ordinary times are the ones that we can never forget even though we are blessed with different ways of remembering them. Ordinary life is the scene and setting for the extraordinary miracles of everyday living, of forgiving each other for our failings, and learning to love each other more, of facing hurt and doubt and setbacks together, of discovering that these are the ways we celebrate the Eucharist of all the living and dying of each ordinary day.

We will learn, as the days turn into weeks, of thousands of ordinary lives and of the freeze frame in which they are now fixed — the goodbyes of husbands and wives, and children, too, heading off on another day, the hundred moments that will forever break our hearts, our chance for goodness and our real glory in being human.

That world was lost with the thousands of the dead, those legions of the ordinary who were so much like us. We will weep for them, as uncomforted as Rachel, and for the ordinary times that were killed with them on Tuesday.

Maybe *This* Is the Greatest Generation

September 18, 2001. America's Baby Boomers recently discovered that their parents — survivors of the Great Depression, winners of World War II — were heroes. What's more, unlike their own constant color commentary on their adventures with Brie and BMWs, their mothers and fathers never talked about what they had endured.

Ever since, these Boomers have paid them honor, in Tom Brokaw's phrase, as "the greatest generation." They have also fingered their guilt like rosary beads at never having faced greater tests than the SATs and whether they would get into the local country club.

Now they have been tested by terror as many headed as a hydra, revealing that, beneath the surface of abs, SUVs, and stock options to which destiny seemed to consign them, they possess at least as much, and maybe more, goodness, heart, and courage as any previous generation.

The thousands of stories set like diamonds in the black heart of this darkness tell us what they may be reluctant to admit: *Theirs* may be the greatest generation ever to grace American life.

The Boomers, some younger and some older, were on the front lines of an attack so savage that nobody could have prepared them for it. The test was raw and fierce, a fulfillment of the scriptural vision of some being taken and others being left, and just so quick as that twinkling of an eye in which all will be changed.

They had nothing to draw on but themselves. And, in that split second of dread, they discovered for themselves the depths of their character, the beauty of their hearts, and the generosity of their souls.

Boomers, critical of their own self-absorption, were tried in the flames that burned away this superficial dross to show how they put away self-concern for the sake of others. Perhaps they learned, as we have learned from them, why their parents never talked about their experiences. When the test came, they stepped out of themselves to find the true north of life as their minds and hearts turned to others. You cannot remember, and so you never talk about, those times when you completely forget yourself.

These Boomers, who seemed so wise about wines and, at times, closer to their black Labradors than to anybody else, found for themselves and showed us where their hearts lay, in those intervals, in airplanes and office buildings, in which they knew that they were going to die.

They also replied to a question asked for centuries but never really answered: What would you do if you knew that the world, or your world, would end in five minutes? A saint was celebrated for looking up from the billiard table and answering that he would go on with his game. But that is, literally, to play, rather than deal, with this proposition.

And who has not heard that, when we know we are about to die, our whole life will flash, MTV style, before our eyes? And how many times have we heard accounts of near-death experiences replete with tunnels, light, and a sense of peace?

But, until September 11, 2001, we had no sample of any size to tell us what people were like when they faced certain death. Now, however, we know, thanks to dozens of cell phone calls and beyond any doubt, what men and women do in these last seconds of their lives.

They forget themselves as they think of those they

love, their spouses and children, their parents and friends. They do not complain or bemoan their fate. Neither do they pray for miraculous deliverance or even for the forgiveness of their sins. They do not think about themselves as they speak their last words.

They just want to tell others how much they love them, that they want them to be safe, that they want them to be happy, that their last will and their true testament is one of utter concern for those they cherish, that they break free of the grasp of death and judgment on their lives by giving themselves away so completely that, before time runs out, they are already immersed in the eternal.

The flaming towers and the skies were not filled with business travelers or tourists that last morning but with lovers, some laying down their lives for their friends, but all of them at their best, drawn fully out of themselves so that we see them as they really were all the time. Blessed are these Boomers, unpossessed by their possessions, saving us rather than themselves, loving their own until the end, as great or greater than any generation we will ever know.

Listen to the Voices of the Ruins

September 25, 2001. Something profound, and not yet well named, has happened to all of us in the last few weeks. Many journalists are stranded on the near shore, stunned by the soaring tide that ravages and reshapes the land they thought they knew. Others, including the comfortless and those who try to comfort them, and maybe most of us, are in the sea itself, bubbles streaming around us as we swim upward from the depths that so suddenly clasped and pulled us down.

We surface on the far reaches of Mystery, at this place as holy as any shrine in the world. If the black boxes of the planes are silent, the hearts of those lost still transmit true signals about what happened to them and to us.

Some claim that myths swirl from the ashes — the water supply is poisoned, the C.I.A. knew about the

bombing all along.[1] "Myth" is the right word used in the wrong way.

"Myth," meaning "falsehood" or "rumor," beggars the human dignity of this event. "Myth," from the Greek for "story," is that way of recounting the truth about us in human tales that are immune to the distortions worked on memory by time and chance.

Myth is also the language of faith. Jesus preached in the mythical form of stories because they are the native tongue of religious mystery. We humans find ourselves, our souls and our destinies, in myths, in the great stories told over and over about the links between love and courage and life and death. The primary significance of the great myths is always spiritual.

That is why people drawn to Ground Zero tell us that no pictures capture its truth. Ground Zero in Manhattan, along with the crater in Pennsylvania and the slashed side of the Pentagon, constitute Ground Sacred. They are now the center of the world of spiritual truth, places where so much seems to be lost but where everything important about us is also found.

Standing silent at the smoking ruins is a greater tribute than placing another wreath of cliches there. We must let this place of Mystery speak to us through its hundreds of stories, each one revealing something different and no two of them the same.

What do we hear if not the *myth,* that is, the *story* of the Hero, that hero, as Joseph Campbell wrote, "with a thousand faces," who stands for all of us who must, some in one way and some in another, pass through the same trial. First, such heroes must leave their own country and journey to one they do not know. There they must face and slay the fiery dragon of ignorance. Only then can they return home with boons for those they left behind.

Everybody who came to work at the World Trade

Center on September 11 made this Hero's Journey. Many were not New Yorkers by birth, and many had come from other parts of the world, leaving behind home, neighborhood, everything and everybody they loved. They came, as bond traders and brokers, secretaries or window washers, to take on the dragon that waits for each of us at every dawn, that beast of what we do not know and cannot fully see that we must daily conquer to be true to ourselves and God's gifts to us.

"Hero" is another word for "saint," for they share a calling, to which the rest of us are apprenticed — to live by the truth of who they are and what they do, thereby slaying the dragon that would feast on them if they were false. Then they can return home, having made themselves whole, another word for holy, through their work that day.

The stories of these hero saints are imperishably invested in the invisible shafts of space that still tower above the ruins: of people journeying every morning on the subways, commuter trains, and airplanes, ready that day for the tests they did not know would be given. These are stories of brothers and sisters, and whole families too, noble hearts seeking the Grail, women weeping as warriors bear dead heroes on their shields, lovers reaching out to that other side of themselves, the beloved who finally made them feel whole; of sons seeking their fathers and fathers seeking their sons and mothers doing the same, every story about people just like us.

They entered the Mystery and defeated the dragon that only seemed to consume them, bearing back to us the priceless spiritual boons of what does and does not count in life. Those asking what to do with this now-sacred place will hear the answer if they listen to these voices of the ruins.

What Judgment Day Is Really Like

October 3, 2001. Since September 11, we have all been on a religious retreat, keeping silence without effort, needing the quiet as we need gentle hands to help us rise after we fall. We have become monks without forsaking the city for the farthest desert and its shimmering heat shield against distraction from the pure presence of God.

We embrace the city where God is purely present to us in the smoking ruins from whose sight we can fashion no distraction. For God is here in these ruins with their towering vigil lights and their wisp of incense smoke, God is here, within the rim of this battered chalice, or God is nowhere.

And, mourning this death in our family, we look differently on many things that we thought we understood. As if we had let the cockle grow with the wheat in our lives, we have come to harvest time and can see

how golden with life are the sheaves of the good crop and how colorless with death the chaff.

In autumnal New York, we can easily differentiate the yields of true religion from those of false religion. Hellfire preachers, lacking all grace and human understanding, have claimed that God struck down the great towers to punish the country for its sensual obsessions and its tolerance of homosexuality. That is the false reaping fit for nothing but to be cut down and burned in the fire.

True religion never adds pain where pain already

overflows. Its gleaning is of understanding, forgiveness, and comfort. Now, seeing the stark difference between these yields, we can see the lives of the lost and dead in perspective, see them, in a way, as God will see all of us on Judgment Day.

We have all been transformed into contemplatives by this horror and may, in this sacred interlude, dismiss once and forever the heavy emphasis that some religions have put on sex as the only or certainly the worst of sins. We can strike the set of the Last Judgment designed by sex-obsessed preachers and prelates as a great stadium on whose giant replay screen your secret thoughts, desires, and sexual fantasies will be flashed, yes, your mother will be there and learn how bad you are before you are waved away to judgment and the next case is called.

We will never believe any of that again. As the yellow-clawed machines squeal their agony and our own and the growling dump trucks bear away everything but memory, we contemplate the sacred lives of the dead. We know that God did not examine, or probably pay much attention to, the sexual feelings they had or the stray carnal images or distractions that flowed through them as they do through all humans.

These dead speak intimately to us about their intimacy, about their loves and friendships, about their work and their play, about what does and does not count in life.

Their voices, taken from phone calls and e-mails and the recollections of friends, blend now into one message, one voice like a canyon echo coming back to us out of the ruins: "I love you," said in a thousand ways, the true harvest of these good people's days. The good grain so overflowed that it covered over the patches of human stubble in their lives.

They defined themselves and what life and faith are all about in their commitment to the *relationships* in their lives. Of what little moment the obscene calls of some preachers to scour out their stray or contrary sexual impulses and to censure them for having sexual temptations or distractions or at times feeling overwhelmed by desire. These are washed away in the tide of love that rose from their hearts as they reached out to their spouses, children, family, and friends.

Once and for all, let us understand that these carnal sparks were footnotes at best in the stories of their lives, summer lightning in the long fruitful season of their years. So they are in the lives of all men and women who are so used to forgetting themselves out of love for others every day that they do it naturally in their last moments. They do it because they have always done it.

Now we understand that the Gospel story about the good and bad seed is really the story of the Last Judgment. What is good and bad in us grows together. On judgment day, God harvests only what is good in us, for that is what is eternal, and ignores the weeds that belong to time.

Neutron Jack and the Jesuit

October 10, 2001. Two men went down to the temple to pray. So begins a Gospel story, as ours does too. The temple, however, is Wall Street, where everybody prayed for the American dream of success. Our parable is told, as all must now be, against the ruins of the World Trade Center, America's broken heart where the sighs of lovers searching for each other will forever fill the air.

One of the men is Jack Welch, the retired head of General Electric, whose book, *Straight from the Gut,* had been widely reviewed on that last peaceful Sunday before September 11. The Sunday *New York Times* editorial had draped a sash on Welch as members do on the departing lodge master who made them happy by balancing the books but happier still by leaving.

The *Times* reflected gingerly on Mr. Welch's style: "His legacy is ... a changed American corporate ethos, one that prizes nimbleness, speed and regeneration over older ideals like stability, loyalty and permanence."

The other man is James Martin, who had given up a successful career on Wall Street to become a Jesuit priest. To much less attention and no editorial notice, his book had also just been published. Its title tells his story: *In Good Company: The Fast Track from the Corporate World to Poverty, Chastity, and Obedience.*

The paper noted that Welch had "earned the nickname 'Neutron Jack' for dismissing 100,000 employees in his early days as chief executive. Rather than dwell on the human cost of such downsizing, Mr. Welch recalls the challenge with relish in his memoir."

Mr. Welch celebrates himself in his pages, noting his parents' influence, especially that of his mother, at whose death he became so angry at God that, in effect, he fired Him from his life. He also apparently applied to the Catholic Church a variant of the slogan he applied to businesses whose operations did not please him, "Fix it, close it, or sell it." He authored a business faith and its first commandment, I am the Lord God of Commerce and you shall not have strange gods before you.

So far, Mr. Welch has had a lot to say about himself but little, if anything, about the terror of September 11. Although his book is number one, he is left, like a figure at Pompeii, fixed and forever forlorn on the far side of the horrific event that seared the gilt off his self-glorification.

Father Martin, now an associate editor at the Jesuit magazine *America,* wrote his book, as he told me, "to show how God can work in people's lives wherever they are, how He can lead persons despite themselves." He has spent the last month ministering to the bereaved and the brave at Ground Zero. "Now," he says, "more important than *how* God works is *that* God works in their lives." He sounds different from Mr. Welch in that he speaks almost wholly of others, saying that "it is an enormous privilege to be with the firefighters and the police where in their unity, concord, and friendship, you feel intensely the presence of the Spirit."

And he speaks of his religious order. "Ground Zero is a good place for Jesuits to be. You pray to Father Pedro Arrupe (later Jesuit Superior General), who ministered in the ruins of Nagasaki after the atom bomb in 1945. These good workers, so happy to see a priest with them, teach you what it means to be a person 'for others.' "

Moving through the grotesque reefs of wreckage, Father Martin hears and sees signs of God everywhere. "In the scripture readings of Sunday about searching for the lost sheep and the woman scouring her house for the lost coin, all these symbolize what these rescue workers are doing. The dayliner boat where they feed them is named *Spirit Cruise,* and when you step on board you find the Kingdom of God. There the firemen, nurses, policemen, and emergency workers sit at the table together in a Eucharistic celebration."

"Grace is everywhere," Father Martin quoted French novelist Georges Bernanos to reassure a young Jesuit co-worker, just as they turned to read in massive letters on the side of a truck, "The Grace Construction Company." Everything, Father Martin says, is a sacrament in this place "where evil has been present and where God is present."

Meanwhile, Mr. Welch says that his only regret is that he didn't fire people sooner. The man who made persons into numbers apparently does not grasp what Father Martin understands. September 11 forever made numbers into people.

Saint Luke's Tooth
and the Trade Towers

October 17, 2001. As St. Paul put it in a different context, a Mystery has been at work in us since the attack of September 11. We feel its pull within us, akin to that of tides and seasons, that we cannot easily name, that yearning to break out of time as innocent prisoners long to break free of their shackles.

That mood has been both broken but also deepened by a dispatch from what seems a distant but parallel universe. A "new DNA analysis," we are told, "gives tentative support to the belief that the remains in an ancient lead coffin are those of St. Luke ... the author of the third Gospel and the Acts of the Apostles."[2]

Population geneticist Guido Barbujani of Italy's University of Ferrara "extracted DNA from a tooth in the coffin [and] ... concluded that the DNA was characteristic of people living near the region of Antioch

...where Luke is said to have been born." Barbujani modestly says that "there is no way to tell if it was the Evangelist Luke but the genetic evidence does not contradict the idea." In a favorite Italian saying, if it isn't a true relic, it ought to be.

This whole story seems written in the subjunctive by a lawyer wary of lawsuits, while the journeys of St. Luke's body, with and without his head (both Prague and Rome once claimed to have the real one), invite skepticism if not satire. Yet, like the tooth itself, its genetic material is profoundly human and is found in every one of us.

For, in lower Manhattan's still smoking hell field, men are searching for human remains, and, at the Fresh Kills site on Staten Island to which the rubble is borne, "wearing white protective suits and masks, agents rake through the debris or watch it roll by on conveyor belts, picking out by hand anything that might be important."[3]

They look for anything that might identify or belong to an individual so that they may bring something definite out of the dusty void to grieving families. People, we learned from the return of remains of those lost in Vietnam, find peace and consolation from the recovery of even fragments of their loved ones. How profoundly human and therefore sacred is this careful exploration of the debris. How richly human, and therefore revealing of ourselves, are the reactions of the workers.

In the room where they don what are white vestments for this liturgy of search and expectation, "a display shows photos of people whose remains have been found...with a brief description of how they were identified. A left hand provided fingerprints that matched those of a police officer; another man's mandible fit with his dental records."

They comb the debris for things, too. They want the flight recorders that, against heavy odds, might bear air speeds and altitudes but, much more valuable, human voices. Detective Carmela "Spike" Cutolo of the New York Police Department found "a miniature license plate, all bent up, with the name Mandy. She hung it on one of the wooden racks where officers lean their rakes and shovels. Some of these racks have become makeshift shrines, decorated with personal effects the officers . . . can't bear to leave in the pile . . . small teddy bears covered with dust and a string of rosary beads."

And so our stories intersect exactly at that point where time dissolves into the eternal, that boundary on which we all now live. It is the geological fault of our humanity, that crevice that lies beneath our everyday seemingly homely activity.

Our human spiritual destiny is to build bridges across that divide so that we may reach and embrace each other. It is that great impulse for communion with each other that opens us to the sacredness of life and our lives together.

We learned on the same day of a body — whether Luke's or not makes no difference — buried lovingly hundreds of years ago and a child's nameplate placed tenderly on a makeshift shrine this week. These are the same story, complete with a family picture that shows our resemblance to each other. There is nothing more human or more divine about us than our longing to touch and hold on to each other. Relics and shrines do not bespeak superstition but rather immortality.

Detective Cutolo spoke for all of us as she searched, "...you don't want to stop. You want to find something so bad, because you want it to be of value to someone."

What Makes Anything Sacred?

October 24, 2001. Sacredness, like holiness, always comes from within human beings. The foundations of sacred places are never in land but rather in deep human experience. Sacredness blooms where people are not thinking about themselves, when, for the sake of others, they let go of everything they might save for themselves. Sacredness cannot be willed but only loved into existence.

We have learned about sacredness ever since Death or the Devil tried to fit New York City with a smoky shroud on September 11, as if, blinded, the metropolis could be claimed by the netherworld. Death and the Devil are cursed because, never having shed lovers' tears, they could not grasp their power to cleanse our vision so that we see more, not less, of the sacred in our lives.

Manhattan is not Sodom and anybody who gazes

back at it is not turned to salt but is granted a vision of the sacred. And New Yorkers beyond counting have turned out to be saints. The city's glitter layer of madness and desire, yes, and seeming sinfulness, burned off quickly to reveal the simple goodness of its ordinary people.

New York is a hearth of the spirit on which, out of human experience rather than theological or political theory, we are forging anew symbols of the Mystery that is within and beyond us at the same time. We are getting a master lesson in what makes things sacred.

The doctor may certify our health, but the doctor does not create it. The pope may proclaim to cheering outdoor crowds that certain men and women are saints. They, however, achieved their holiness internally, out of the sight of great crowds, to no applause at all.

When he blesses a new church, a bishop knows that it will ultimately be made sacred by the people who bring their experience of never-ending dying and rising to its altar. The holiness floods in on the tide of their lives. They are unaware that they bring it because it flows from their forgetting themselves to take care of others.

First, we recognize that something sacred has occurred in a certain location, on France's World War I battlefield at Verdun, or in the simple Chicago quarters of America's first saint, Mother Cabrini. We sense that people were alive to each other here, that they forgot themselves and loved and laid down their lives for each other in this place. That is the source of the sacredness.

Manhattan has been washed in the blood of the lamb, and Ground Zero is sacred because its ruins are imbued with the mystery of the lives that were lived there. This is our century's *Titanic*, this shipwrecked vessel from whose passengers, crew, and rescuers we learn more every day about what makes anything sacred. How could we miss it? How can we not eat and drink of this profound sacrament?

The shock of its impact must explain why New York's Cardinal Edward Egan could gaze on the ruins through an outdated theological lens and see the human person and the world as divided into a lesser, strictly secular level and a separate and higher sacred plane. "I did see a tremendous amount of holiness that may have been secular," he said, "but it may have been pushing into the supernatural, the spiritual."[4]

In his heart, New York's pastor knows better because he has allowed scores of fire and police personnel to be buried with "Danny Boy" sung, or played on bagpipes, an air made sacred by their sacrifice, at their funerals. Timing was unkind to Robert Mulvee, bishop of Providence, who, before September 11, had banned this ballad from funerals as non-liturgical music.[5]

But what makes a melody of loss and longing fit for a liturgy if not that it captures, as the flag does the wind, the goodness of those who embrace their duty and their destiny as so many did on September 11?

The cardinal understands that grace is not borne in a drone plane tracking our lives that, if we remember to contact it with the right password, beams down sacred rays to us. Nobody who has seen the sacred ruins can imagine that a dividing line of natural and supernatural ran across those who died there, or runs across those who work heroically there. We sense them as whole and, therefore, holy.

If we cannot see the intrinsic sacredness of Ground Zero, that symbol of life-as-it-is-lived — wholeheartedly, imperfectly, tragically — then we do not get it and will never understand what makes anything and everything sacred.

All Saints Day/All Souls Day

October 31, 2001. "When disaster strikes," Joseph Campbell once asked, "...what is it that supports you and carries you through?...That is the test of myth, the building myth of your life."[6]

We stand together, commanded into silence by the ruins of the Trade Towers where the guiding myths, or religious and spiritual convictions, were tested. Smoke, a mythical, sacramental element, changes the air just as oil, another sacramental element, transforms the water above the sunken battleship *Arizona* at Pearl Harbor. These symbols reach that level of profound and mysterious currents — the smoke riding on the breath of the spirit, and the oil on the depths from which its healing stream flows. They sing together of the legendary elements of all life — earth, air, fire, and water.

In this jagged amphitheater that has become the center of our world, the lost also speak to us, less of their deaths than of their lives, in which all the spiritual elements that matter may be identified.

We hear the roll call of generations so often sounded in the Bible, of Timothy Haskell, who had three firemen brothers, and of fireman Daniel Suhr with a father and brother in the department. And Chris Kirby, nicknamed "Happy," who wanted to be a fireman like his father. Thomas Hannafin followed his brother Kevin into the Fire Department, and it was

Kevin who found his body and carried his helmet out of the wreckage.

Robert Curatolo, with one brother a policeman and one a firefighter, dragged a man out of one of the buildings to safety. A photograph survives, a blurred gift of the spirit, allowing us to see him heading back into the building along with many others, to lay down their lives.

There were also sisters, like twenty-four-year-old Samantha and thirty-one-year-old Lisa Egan, who worked at the same firm. They would be trying to find each other, their father said. And siblings, like twenty-five-year-old Khamadar and twenty-one-year-old Rosan Singh, the only children of their widowed mother, working at a breakfast meeting. Yamel Marino, twenty-one, stands for all single mothers, just as João Aguilar does for all young lovers. "For the first time in his life," we are told, "he was in love."

Fireman Timothy Stackpole testifies for all those men who had just finished their shifts but felt it was their duty to go to the scene. And let William Wik speak for those who thought it was their duty to remain. He rejected his wife's urging him to leave,

"No, I can't do that, there are still people here." And allow Frank Doyle and Robert Parks, Jr., to represent all the fathers of small children, all those who coached their teams and bathed them and put them to bed, and left their cars at suburban railway stations to speak as poignantly as the abandoned ships of Arctic explorers.

And what do we overhear on the party line of all the cell phone calls? Something finer and rarer than panic or regret. Their first thoughts became last words as they sought out those they loved. Veronique Bowen called her grandmother and her mother, "There is smoke everywhere, I'm trapped, I love you." And Norman Rossimov, thirty-nine, calming his wife, "If you tell me you love me, I'll come home."

Lawrence Virgilio, thirty-eight, who once trained in classic ballet, speaks for all those who were planning to marry. He called, his girl friend said, to "tell me that he loved me." Eamon McEneany of Cantor Fitzgerald left a message with his wife's assistant, "Tell Bonnie that I love her, that I love the children, that I'm on my way out."

What is more touching or more familiar than time choking the eternal impulse to reach a loved one? The phone records reveal that Yvonne Bonomo dialed her mother at 8:51 a.m. on that day but that the call never got through.

John Mark Dingle did not get to say goodbye to his wife, but it was learned that he had brought her ring to a jeweler to have a larger diamond placed in it. Everybody knew sixty-five-year-old Mon Gionbali as "Jambalaya." He called his family, "I'm trapped, I don't think I'm going to see you guys again. Keep the family together. Keep strong."

And Louie Anthony Williams did what we would all yearn to do. "He just liked to let you know that you are loved," his wife said afterward, and he was always leaving notes on her pillow. Every morning he would e-mail her in code. 381 meant "I love you." After the plane struck, he sent another, 38114, "I love you forever."

Let the Living Bury Their Dead

November 7, 2001. The site where the Trade Towers stood is America's Calvary where the still unfathomable loss of September 11 breeds deeper losses and the first sorrow issues into intense secondary sorrows as, in repeated images of the Pietà, mothers and sons wait for their loved ones to be taken down from their place of death so that they may cradle them in their arms and bear them home.

This second wave of pain was also felt when heroes of the New York Fire Department were arrested by heroes of the New York Police Department after venting their grief in protests at the foot of Manhattan's Golgotha.[7]

These aftershocks offer us a measure of how deep is our loss and of how little we comprehend it. It will take us a long time to begin to grasp how its rage and mystery work beneath and beyond our words

to symbolize or command them. Such red raw pain mocks our culture's efforts to hurry sorrow as if it were sundown so that we can achieve "closure" on it.

We cannot "deal with" this event. We can only respond to it, and that requires us to enter this mystery of loss. That is the message of the firefighters who protested the city's limiting the number of them who could be present at the site. Such a decree, designed, it was said, for safety, cut into something deeper than workplace regulation.

This scene, causing fresh pain for everybody connected with this tragedy, tells us how profound are our needs after we have suffered enormous loss. So deep is this wound to our spirit that we humans can only express it symbolically, through carrying out rituals as old as honor itself.

Nothing is more human than our need to do that work of mourning that nobody can do for us. We cannot interrupt this spiritually and psychologically necessary work without damaging those who are carrying it out. It is not unusual, we are told by experts, for those in mourning to search symbolically for a lost spouse or child. This activity appears irrational and perhaps even wasteful or dangerous from our point of view but, for those who mourn, it is an essential activity if they are going to complete this labor, as great as any of Hercules and as old as any we know.

Those who interrupt or try to manage mourning always have good reasons — safety or that need for "closure" — so they do not understand how they are endangering the mourners when they interrupt their carrying out this ancient and sacred work.

That is why the New York firefighters scuffled with the police. The river of loss batters against the artificial dams set up to contain or divert it, overruns its banks to flow where it will. Listen as these mourning firefighters tell us of the work of mourning only they can do.

"Bring our brothers home," they shout, referring to the 250 firemen still lying beneath the rubble. "You can't treat sacred ground," one says, "as just another construction site." Mike Heffernan speaks "of the great relief that comes when a family recovers the body of a loved one...as he did on October 1 when the remains of John Heffernan, his brother, and a firefighter, were found and buried."

As Fire Captain Bill Butler speaks, you can hear the keening in the souls of all the generations of parents over their children taken by death, "My son Tommy from Squad 1 is still in that building and we haven't gotten him yet." And in the background, voices welled out of the deep mystery, "Bring Tommy home, bring the brothers home...."

Larry Mooney speaks for them all, "They want to pull out the people with cranes. We want to bring back our brothers with dignity.... We've got friends and brothers and family. This goes very deep."

So deep that we need to give everyone time and space in which to grieve and allow them to do it in their own way and on their own schedule. Reporters at the memorial service held at the site found their own superficiality revealed by the depths of those searching in that desperate place for those they loved.

"Why had they come here today to this difficult place,... [a] correspondent asked the woman whose husband was...killed on September 11." She had to come here, came the swift, agonized answer. "I had to breathe the air — I had to fill up my lungs with him."[8]

The Site

November 14, 2001. We have learned again that we have not yet found the words to express, even to ourselves, Fate's rape and murder of New York City. "Unreal city," T. S. Eliot wrote in *The Waste Land*, "...I had not thought death had undone so many."

Listen, then to what the police, fire, and emergency personnel tell us. They are reluctant to describe the Trade Center wreckage as "Ground Zero."

They call it "The Site." They did not select this by vote or poll but by discovering that the phrase expresses what they feel but cannot yet fully name about these seared and sacred acres.

"Site" is as rich in meanings as Manhattan's lapping waters are with salt and memory. "Site" may seem a general description of a place or location. Yet it carries meanings like a flag. We sense these in its Latin verb of origin: *sinere,* "to leave, to allow to remain."

This Amish-plain designation unearths an edge of the true feelings buried deep inside the workers who, as we say, tend the site. The horror of September 11 may resonate in "Ground Zero," but its spiritual reality buds like a wasteland flower out of "The Site."

We speak respectfully of an "archeological site," that space set aside because it contains the everyday things of people who lived before us but not unlike us. We feel a kinship with them at the hearths where they gathered, as hungry for food and story as we, and in the sprays of now-withered flowers they placed with their dead to express a tenderness and love that make them cousins to us all. We protect such places from careless passage or violation because we recognize our family resemblance to those who once breathed and worked and yearned for love there.

"Site" is medicine's word for the place in the body where the blow was struck, the *wound* suffered. "Site" also refers to the place at which the fertilized egg attaches itself to the *womb*. "The Site" speaks to us of the *wound* and the *womb*, of a place of suffering that may lead to death and of a place of joining that is the beginning of life.

"The Site" is our Atlantis, this great place, silent although filled with sound, alive although filled with death, pure as only human hearts can be even in air fouled by the dust devils that are watered into grayish mud by the roving sprinkler trucks that stir memories of the long-lost peace of summer streets.

The mood of loss fills this great amphitheater of wreckage as Tchaikovsky's *Pathetique* symphony pervades a concert hall. For if much has been removed, much remains. Great sections of buildings hang open like battered car doors, their contents exposed in jagged tiers, a freeze frame of their occupants' last moments so poignant that it seems sacrilegious to gaze at it.

"The Site" is our Coventry, a war-destroyed cathedral with a charred spire of tower facing propped in its wreckage. Around it, as in an ancient town square, huddle the structures that received savage secondary damage. Here are the scarred and boarded shops and schools, hotels and lesser office buildings, many of which will come to life again, much as we will, the same and yet never the same.

At the center of "The Site" energy wrestles with loss like Jacob with the angel of death. Here the confident muscularity of America is at work lifting out the debris beneath the swaying white booms of the birds of prey machines, as majestic as the ruins themselves. Nearby stand the trucks, bareheaded and silent, the pallbearers waiting to carry away the tower remains.

And American organization is everywhere, in the tents in which the workers eat, and others in which they bathe, and others, as lively as those in an oil patch boomtown, filled with everything, from fresh socks to a few moments of friendliness, and from new boots to rubdowns for these valiant harvesters of the overwhelming grief and loss.

One grieves for New York, its suffering placed almost beyond grief by the crash of another plane into a neighborhood that had already offered its sacrifice to this darkest of autumns. Perhaps the only fitting thing that the New York Yankees could bring back from the World Series was loss, rather than noisy victory, to lay as a wreath of honor at "The Site."

Listen, then, to the scripture for a Sunday in this season: *Today salvation has come to this house for this is what it means to be a son of Abraham. The Son of Man has come to search and save what was lost.*

Revelations at Thanksgiving

November 21, 2001. At Thanksgiving we stand on the ridge, lighted palely by the fleeing sun, just above the dark, chill valley of winter. We have usually made our accounting with the year by now, knowing, as the farmers do, of the land now sealed until spring, how to count our blessings and mark where we stand with life.

This year, we are certain only that we are still absorbing the blow, that it will ache like a healing bone within us through the snowy sleep of winter, and that its pain, but not its Mystery, may be less when spring's first light rises.

Still, a blessing is not the same as good luck. Blessings are never a bargain and are paid for in the currency minted in the soul by our surrender of something we have been holding back of ourselves.

Good luck, conversely, may be as cheap as a lottery

ticket or as morally expensive as insider trading. If it adds to our bank account, it also increases our fear of losing it, and we begin to screen people better than airport guards to protect what we have and hide who we are. Such fear, the scriptures tell us, casts out love.

On this first Thanksgiving after September 11, we may count as a blessing big enough for the nation what we learned about so many people who died that day. They were good at love, we learn, and, in their last minutes, they used their love to cast out fear.

They have heaped these blessings onto our tables and, as the scripture says again, into our laps, full measure, shaken down, and running over. Blessed are they, and we through them, who thought not of themselves but of others and laid down their lives for them.

We may offer thanks that the Age of Revelation, said to have closed with the death of the last of Jesus' apostles, has been reopened in our time. "Revelation" comes from the word that means "unveiling." "Apocalypse" also means "unveiling."

Scourges are the opposite of blessings, and we know more about them now as well. Mythically and spiritually, scourges always slay love and beauty. They reveal in their thousand tactics — as in the Nazis breaking up Jewish families the better to breed terror — that if love is killed, the beauty of life is slain as well.

September 11 was a day not to destroy towers dedicated to trade as much as to massacre the lovers as individuals, marked as plainly as hospitals by their good hearts, along with their families, their children, the simple times they savored, and, finally, life itself. For these lovers breathed their spirits into the buildings, as Jesus did into the sick and dying, to bring them alive and to reveal their beauty at every dawn.

If the event was an *apocalypse,* it was even more an *unveiling.* It is true that apocalypse seemed victorious as the curtain walls of the Trade Center fell into fountains of debris and dust dark enough to rob the day of the sun. So, too, its scourging horsemen seemed triumphant at the flaming Pentagon and in the scorched Pennsylvania meadow.

The apocalypse betrayed its own monstrosity by unveiling the beauty of those it destroyed. Seeking to rob them of time, it revealed what was eternal about them. Those who seemed lost have instead been found, and the simple beauty of their ordinary lives has been made into an imperishable blessing for us.

Our eyes have been opened because their tongues have been loosed and they speak to us every day of values we thought long decertified by the postmodern world. Their stories are blessings of reassurance not because they are so different from but because they are so like our own or those of our own families.

These men and women bless us by confiding in us. Some tell us again their own version of *Beauty and the Beast,* while still others help us to understand the true meaning of the apocalyptic phrase "the End of the World."

They tell us stories of how, on meeting, often, by surprise, something was unveiled for them as they suddenly saw in each other a beauty so rare as to be saved for their eyes alone and so great as to tame the ranging beast of loneliness in that moment. Their *world came to an end*, not through apocalyptic destruction but because their love allowed them to see together what they could not see alone, the infinite beauty of the world they now shared with each other.

And so an old world has come to an end for us as well, and we count at Thanksgiving the ordinary human blessings whose power terror revealed but could not destroy.

The Mountains at the Center of the World

November 28, 2001. Advent heralds Christmas and means "arrival," or "to come to." This year we have already arrived, at *the center* rather than *the end of the world.*

For here, in lower Manhattan, made as poor as Bethlehem by terrorists, we cluster at that still point in the spiritual universe where there is no turning. Every spiritual journey must now pass through this space where every day the bones of Golgotha are overturned, the temple of Jerusalem falls, and Jesus bids the bandaged Lazarus to come forth from his tomb.

Interior growth, once described as a "spiritual combat," is really an *odyssey* that requires passage through such places of trial. So the Jews wandered in the desert and St. Paul found himself "in journeying often," and

that he had to enter a "door open and evident" to fulfill his calling.

In the Bible, we hurry through the gates that groan as they close behind us. Some are figurative, such as the gates of hell, and some are spiritual, guarded by angels bearing flaming swords, while still others are as real as the great gate of Jerusalem through which Jesus passes on a jolting donkey to shouted blessings and waving palms. The Good Shepherd tells us that we must enter the sheepfold through the Gate. And Jesus says simply, "I am the Way."

In the testaments, mountains almost outnumber gates, some so steep that clouds envelop Moses as God hands him the tablets of the commanded life, and others so gentle in slope that the five thousand can see Jesus as he feeds them and reveals the simplicity of the blessed life.

Great mystics, such as Teresa of Avila and John of the Cross, describe their calling as an ascent on the mount of perfection. Yet this, too, is a mysterious journey, for John inscribes on the summit the words "there is no way here." And St. Peter is told by Jesus of his calling that someone will gird him with a strap and lead him in a way that he would rather not go.

We have been led in a way we would rather not go and have arrived together at the same moment as if in a dream. And so we found ourselves, when it was not yet the ninth hour on September 11, at the center of the world.

Inscribed on this mound of ruin are the mystical words "there is no way here." No way that can be understood by reason, nor a path cleared by another, no way that our entering this experience can be transferred to anyone else.

The biblical mountains cluster here: Ararat, where

the ark rested after the flood, and Pisgah, from which Moses viewed the Promised Land, the mount of the Transfiguration, that of the Beatitudes, that of Calvary, a spiritual range rising above the foothills of twisted wreckage.

We understand this place better through the counterpart mythical vision of Sioux Chief Black Elk. He spoke of South Dakota's Harney Peak as "the earth mountain, the center of the world.... This vast tipi seemed to be as large as the world itself.... The peoples that were there in that lodge, they talked to me."[9]

And so they speak to us, here where the smoke pennants stream day and night. We hear the good shepherd police and fire rescuers calling to each other, and to us, as they seek the sheep that are lost. Yes, and *the peoples that were in that lodge, they speak to us,* too, of the simple goodness of their lives.

Blessed are they who loved their work and their spouses and hurried home to play with their children and put them to bed. Blessed are those who thought always of others and were transported, as in a biblical chariot, into the exploding clouds. Blessed are those who, facing death, forgot themselves, and were last seen "going back into the building," "making sure others got on the elevator," "returning to be sure everyone else had left."

Michael Trinidad, who had reached the mystical age of thirty-three, tells us how to heal what seems broken. He phoned his former wife, "I love you and I love the kids. I'm not going to make it out." Then he asked to speak to her new husband, bidding him to be "my children's father and to love them for me."[10]

We are all spiritual immigrants who arrived by the same gate, past the angels with the flaming swords, to find that the Kingdom of God has suffered violence. It has not been borne away but delivered to us at this wounded site that is the center of the spiritual world.

Happy the Sorrowing
for They Have Known Love

December 5, 2001. Heartbreak so took over the world in September that the year is dying of it, "of natural causes," let the obituaries read, rather than of calendar dates or cosmological destiny. For as natural as love and its immeasurable gains are to humans, just as natural are suffering and its all too easily measured losses. They are the two sides of the currency of everyday life, the love we seem accidentally to earn and the sorrow with which we seem unfairly charged.

Heartbreak is impossible unless there is great love. In December's lowering light, we see the precious revelations purchased at the price of terrible loss. In a year still feeling the aftershocks of hate everywhere, we find that love is everywhere, too.

Love is the invisible aura and energy of ordinary life. We can see it better now in the unself-conscious and the unsung who died in September but who still sit next to us on trains and airplanes, the men and women who seem so impassive on their commuting and business trips.

Indeed, we have been warned about them. Behold, the clergy, the commentators, and even the pope advise us, here is the pure strain of *Consumer Americanus,* sex-absorbed and money-mad, first citizens of a *culture of death*, squanderers of the world's resources, destroyers of family life and sources of poverty and injustice everywhere else.

When we get a good look at them, is that what we see?

They are our surrogates in this rehearsal for our own judgment where we will arrive, as they did, in the midst of strangers, each ending long and different journeys that converge at the same place in the same moment.

We also understand better biblical phrases and themes that have seemed abstract, static tableaux from another time. We sense, as the followers of Jesus did on the road to Emmaus, that the Lord had been walking, unrecognized, with them on their journey.

We were all granted a mystical vision and, in the twinkling of an eye, we understood at last the "signs in the heavens" prophesied in the Book of Revelation. For as the towers and planes were wrenched brutally apart, the lives of ordinary people were gently opened for us.

We were allowed to glimpse this cross-section of humanity, come from every continent to this last morning, to see them just as they were, as, at their day's beginning, they stepped into the elevators and sat down at their desks. And we were able to watch others who, at their shift's ending, climbed back onto the fire trucks or into their police cars to take their places in a religious revelation that breaks and elevates our hearts.

We understand the apocalyptic language of a lightning flash passing from one end of the sky to another. It is not a slashing dagger of punishment for human folly but the light, gentle as a bedside candle, that lifts away the shadows that obscure human good.

Happy the pure of heart, we read in the book of Matthew, for they shall see God. And, perhaps for the first time, we understand purity of heart and what it allows people to see.

Many of us fear that the spotlight of judgment will shame us by revealing the flaws we have tried to hide from others or the secret sins we have kept to ourselves. But September's sudden judgment burned away these surface faults to reveal the purity in the hearts of these men and women who loved as best they could their families and friends. They lived face to face, we learn in their stories, and so they were ready to see God face to face as well.

This is no small gift from the dying year. We have learned what real spirituality is and that it is found, not at distant shrines, nor in seeking perfection in exile from life, but by staying home in the wondrous imperfection of standard-issue existence.

How like us they were, falling down, getting up, starting over, every day, just as they were on the last day when their paths intersected, in skyscrapers and jet planes. How could we fail to see that these are the "signs in the heavens" to which the Apocalypse alerts us?

Our world dies of sorrow only because it witnesses great love. Without love, sorrow and tears would disappear. There would be no need for them. Let us not miss, as some do, or look away from, as others do, this central spiritual event of our time, this revelation of love and sorrow that sums up the Law and the Prophets.

Closing In on the Caves

December 12, 2001. "Closing In on the Caves," the *New York Times* headline reads, capturing the strange conjunction of our terror and wonder as we close in on Christmas.[11] Very different caves open before us.

Caves speak from their spiritual depths to our own. The cave, Joseph Campbell tells us, "has always been the scene of the initiation, where the birth of light takes place."[12] So, too, the cave stands for "the heart, where the light of the divine first appears." The cave is also associated with "the emergence of light...out of the abyss of the early chaos."

A cave reportedly houses our Herod, Osama bin Laden, smiling as he directs the slaughter of the innocent. Does he now enter our symbolic cave to defile Mother Earth as he did Father Sky with the silver daggers of his highjacked planes?

We are not surprised that Osama bin Laden should make sacrilege of this symbol, as he has of human life, by seeking to use the image of light to camouflage his own dark actions. Nor are we surprised that this master of distant treachery should now profane this cave symbol of the human heart and all our hope with his terror.

Skies and caves, found everywhere in the ancient myths and biblical tales, have been filled with signs for us during this long slow autumn of loss and discovery. For terror fell like lightning from the sky, Lucifer descending after battling the angels for domination of the universe.

Winter's star now rides the sky, guiding our search for the sacred cave at Bethlehem in which, as the sun turns back from its long flight away from us, we find the Light of the World. We are drawn, as Oriental kings once were, to this Bethlehem cave that offers shelter to the young lovers so that hope may be born again in the world.

And we are drawn to other caves, one in lower Manhattan, another in Washington, D.C., and one more in the Pennsylvania mountains. These constitute our Bethlehem this year for, in what we have lost and also found there, we enter the great religious Mystery of our age.

We bring our gifts to the fulness of the cave symbol in the ravaged earth where light flickers "out of the abyss of the early chaos." We ask the same question as the puzzled kings: Why are we summoned here, and what gifts can we lay in these places of loss?

The loss itself is made more forlorn by those who, despite the abundant signs, cannot perceive its spiritual significance, or give a mistaken interpretation to its intrinsic religious Mystery. Like any great wound, that in lower Manhattan is still being gently probed and cleansed. When an effort was made, for safety reasons, to redefine this cave of death as a "construction site," and firemen were greatly restricted in bringing out their dead, all New York shuddered in a reflex of pain.

So the violated earth reacts against those who can only see it as a king's head held up above territory long disputed by war lords, the destined outcome of, and perhaps a punishment for, our own sins, a shadow wound of all those inflicted by American imperialism.

As it is a failure of the readers and not the book if they cannot find the mystery in the Bible, so it is with the three wounds of September, the American stigmata, and the mystery of unutterable pain and loss that they signify. They open our eyes to the nature of religious Mystery itself. That is what the coming of the light symbolizes.

We learn again that religious Mystery can never be found by abandoning what is human in a misconstrued search for the divine. Mother Earth is the only known host for humanity, and humanity is the sole host to religious Mystery.

As astrophysicists and cosmologists intuit a perfect universe on the evidence of the imperfect one they observe, so we find ultimate religious Mystery in these cave wounds in which the loving hearts of the lost have been laid open to us.

Our approach is slow work, much like that at this cave of many entrances at Ground Zero. There, goggled and helmeted searchers are the royalty from the Orient, bearing the gift of themselves, defeating the darkness with their light, moving carefully as if conscious that they are searching inside a symbol for the heart. They enter the tangle of loss for remains but they emerge bearing whole lives.

They are attendants at the birth of religious Mystery. As scientists glimpse a perfect universe in the broken one before their eyes, the discoveries of these searchers allow us to see the perfection of religious Mystery in the seemingly broken and unfinished lives of these parents and children and family and friends.

We close in on a cave, not that of terrorists' flight, but the cave that is the symbol of light and heart, the cave of Bethlehem and the caves of September 11.

The Christmas Mystery
of the World As It Is

December 19, 2001. We are worn out from looking on the suffering of this year that is now dying with no last words, this long school term of daily examinations less on what we have learned than on whether we have learned anything at all, this long prison sentence in which time passes while it also stands still. "Yes, we have gone on living," many feel with T. S. Eliot, "living and partly living."

Those words, from *Murder in the Cathedral*, match the sense that the year challenges some central American longings. We love mysteries but also want them solved immediately. The idea that some mysteries cannot be solved, are forever beyond us, is disquieting. We protect ourselves against mystery by donning earphones, passing through museums more like drone planes than art lovers, never allowing the paintings

to speak directly to, and possibly disturb, our own depths.

Our mystery-intolerance makes us obsessed with "closure," with capping our experiences the way Americans cap burning oil wells, terminating the flaming overflow of such mysteries as death and loss. Some say that we need "closure" on the thousands of deaths out of due time we have seen this year, or otherwise their meaning may forever elude us and our mourning never be done.

These frustrated and frustrating longings are aspects of a larger engulfing drama of human experience in which we all have speaking parts. We suffer together the suffering world, that "stained glass," as the poet put it, "on the white radiance of existence."

We continue to witness this ongoing Mystery that will not be solved even when its planners and perpetrators have been apprehended, found guilty, and punished. That is the easy part of this Mystery that is the *sacramentum mundi,* the sacrament of our world, the symbol reflecting the image of the world back to it and to us.

"Myth," as most of us understand, does not mean a false notion but rather refers to events that symbolize basic and abiding human truths in ways, such as stories, that make them immune to the superficial changes wrought by time and chance.

The attacks of September 11 constitute, before our eyes and in our hearts, a mythical event in a myth-starved era, a tragic yet mystical orchestration of human experience that we enter, without explanation, solution, or hope of closure, to discover and recognize the Mystery of being.

No other current event so captures the unfathomable character of our existence together, *as we are* in *the world as it is.* The "religious function of a mythology, that is, the mystical function" Joseph Campbell reminds us, "... represents the discovery of the dimension of the mystery of being."[13]

Christmas is a mythical event whose story will outlast time's variations and history's vandals. It will even survive the ACLU because it tells us our story, the great human story we recall at the peak of every year.

God once looked at His creation and found that it was good. But Christmas tells us that God entered *the world as it is,* our world, the same imperfect, pain-, injustice-, and sin-filled world that lies about us, this vast, tragic wonder of love and goodness ever terrorized by loss and death.

The trinity of September 11 attacks reveal, as nothing has since the Holocaust, *the world as it is,* this Mystery we can never solve, abounding in sins and flaws that reformers never understand and can never extinguish, the pain and sorrow from which we are never free, and the love, ever outweighed and overmatched, that thrives on this imperfection is found only in this imperfection, the love that makes life possible and conquers death itself.

9/11 symbolizes the religious Mystery of our being.

How unlike an angelic choir we are. In this mythical event we find everything that has ever happened in human history, every language spoken, every emotion of the heart, every age group, every degree of education, every state of health from the gym-minted fit to the handicapped, every longing and every hurt, every dream and every delusion, every hope and every kind of plan, the timid and the brave, yes, and, above all and in everyone, sparks enough of love and self-forgetfulness to redeem it all — in James Joyce's words, "Here Comes Everybody."

As the next of kin, we cannot ignore this Mystery. How could we miss the family resemblance and fail to recognize the Christmas religious mystery we can never solve, of our lives *as we are* in *the world as it is?*

Cardinal Mahony, Mayor Giuliani, and the Numbers Game

January 1, 2002. The secular rites for 2001 are lists composed of figures: Who is Number One? Which are the Ten Best? What is the closing Dow Jones average? How much was the Christmas Collection?

Each question tries to quantify elements that squirm away like mercury under the measurer's probe. Can we paint by the numbers a graph of whether, after September 11, religion's *influence* rose or declined in people's lives?

The renowned Pew Research Center for the People and the Press asked, "Aside from weddings and funerals how often do you attend religious services ... more than once a week, once a week, once or twice a month, a few times a year, seldom, or never?"

But these resemble the questions of reporters after any disaster: "How did you feel when your house burned down?" This curiosity kills cats but confounds the surface with the substance of how we experience or manifest religion in our lives.

Cardinal Roger Mahony of Los Angeles responded by noting that religion is better recognized in the way people live their ordinary lives, raise their families, and do their work.

New York's outgoing Mayor Rudolph Giuliani reminded us in his last talk that the place where so many died is *sacred ground* that must be preserved because its value can never again be summed up in the price per square foot of a new commercial building.

The cardinal and the mayor understand that religious Mystery is found not by doing the math but by entering the Mystery that is fundamentally and fully celebrated not inside but outside houses of worship, in the neighborhoods, homes, and workplaces of men and women faithful to their callings. People don't find religion in church; they bring faith there so that it can be liturgically symbolized and they can be nourished in order to go in peace, as the celebrant says, to love and serve the world.

We are still seeking words for what can never be numbered, the great Mystery of Revelation, as blinding and as beyond calculation as sunrise, that we entered together in September. This Mystery, like the biblical God, dwells beyond all names and all numbering. We can only contemplate it.

Now we have pushed our skiff off from the old year as from an island to which we will never return. We gaze back as we seek the slipstream to the open sea, our feelings at odds as the waters are with each other at the turning of the tide.

The year and the island are Manhattan, of course, and, as we see them in better perspective, we sense that, for these places and for us, some fateful moment has come to a close if not to an end. We hardly knew ye, we lament, as the mourning Irish do of the mythical Johnny, symbol of the losses borne by the land and the year that we can no longer enter and can never quite leave.

The deep water on which we drift is our unconscious, that limitless space of the spirit within each of us. We need not plumb it completely to feel its pull as we cup it in our hands. Taste and see that it is as rich in religious Mystery as the ocean is in salt and the stuff of life. Where else could we have come from if not this home of life's infinite mystery?

As we move farther from this island, this kingdom of God within the living and the lost, we understand why families and friends cannot separate themselves from these places where their loved ones lie. We also grasp why New York City has built viewing platforms near the site of the World Trade Towers, for our eyes will never be filled with the looking that is essential to our taking possession of this experience while letting go of it at the same time.

Are we Americans just *consumers* when we realize that we cannot *consume* this event, and that we will never *exhaust* it? It is the vessel of oil never diminished, the Eucharist ever on our table, to which we attend in ways that, as both Cardinal Mahony and Mayor Giuliani know, can never be counted. In the new year we discover a calling we never expected, to stand in the choir stalls of everyday, where neither rust nor moth nor pollster may enter, and *contemplate* in our own time this eternal Mystery.

The Pain inside Pain

January 16, 2002. The World Trade Center site is now a vast mine, resembling the terraced depths in Butte, Montana, from which fathers and sons once extracted freight-car loads of copper beyond counting. Ground Zero has now yielded a million tons of wreckage and, as the *New York Times* observes, "a million tons of pain."[14]

Firemen and policemen search there every day, lost themselves in their longing to find the sons and brothers who vanished into the sky on September 11 like the prophet Elijah. As deep as this dig goes into the earth, just so deep it goes into the hearts of those waiting at the mine head for word of those they love.

That we may close our eyes or our ears against this Mystery of Loss measures the layers it has laid open in us. The chalice of suffering is being passed along, as the debris buckets first were, from hand to hand, from inside the fallen towers, from within the inexhaustible Mystery itself, take this and drink from it. . . .

When we accept this cup we dissolve the theological wrangles about whether members of different religions may share the sacraments together. So argue institutions that, relishing power, do not understand love or how it arises when suffering is shared. It is in the breaking of the bread and drinking of the vessel of this sorrow that we take communion together.

Sorrow teaches us that we belong to the same family, that we are next of kin to everyone waiting at this mine of suffering. Retired Fire Department captain John Vigiano, sixty-three, is there every day. The body of his police detective son, Joseph, thirty-four, was found in October, but that of his thirty-six-year-old fireman son, John, has not yet been recovered. "When I sit down there alone," the father says, "I talk to him and tell him I love him."

And forty-one-year-old Brian Lyons quit his job to work at the site so that he could look for his brother, Michael, whose recently recovered ID card he carries. "I know he's talking to me," he says. "He's saying, 'Brian, don't quit. I'm in here.'"

These words consecrate all loss and suffering,

piercing time as carefully and cleanly as the shovels do the ashes of the ruins. Closure is a false god here where sorrow can engulf us as earth does when searching touches off a landslide. Drink this cup and learn the terrible truth that suffering may harbor other sufferings within itself.

This is the collateral damage, the terrible small problems unshelled from the larger one. Long Island priest Father James Lisante responds to secondary damage when parents and the victim's spouse disagree on decisions, opening old wounds — was she ever good enough for him, or who is he to make these decisions anyway?

Add the anguish of those lost along the paper trail to compensation from the funds set up to help them. Trial lawyers, overcoming their initial moratorium on suing, do not recognize the side-effect pain and suffering of their supposed legal remedies for pain and suffering.

We feel the red raw inner lining of this pain in the heartfelt reactions of relatives to plans to build again at the site forever sacred to them. We feel it when these same mourners are wounded by souvenir makers who fashion a business out of their loss. There is a terrible pain at the viewing platforms between those who feel drawn spiritually to this space and those relatives who feel that their dead are violated by the eyes of such pilgrims. Inner chambers of pain open on still other ones when a sculpture of firemen raising the flag on the first day is cast not in bronze but in a lime bath of controversy.

Some spiritual traditions say that we must gradually numb ourselves to the world, that we must meditate or chant ourselves into a blessed indifference to its joys and sorrows and, thus armored against delight in gain or suffering in any loss, preserve an airless space of peace within ourselves.

Perhaps that was Eden's temptation — to escape the Mystery rooted at its center from the beginning. How else explain a tree bearing the fruit of the knowledge of good and evil? Perhaps our first parents rebelled at what they learned and we now discover, that good and evil, along with sorrow and joy and their secondary growths, are inter-mingled in our lives, that we never find one without the other.

Lower Manhattan will be filled in one day but we will mine the Mystery of September 11, necessarily inlaid with both loving and suffering — *Our Mystery* — all the days of our lives.

Lost/Found/Learned

February 16, 2002. The recently released police helicopter videos of September 11 record the real beginning of this century.

Seeded into the gray riptide of debris engulfing the streets and impounding the life of lower Manhattan is the Mystery of Loss that is lodged now, like radiation, in our souls. We speak of loss in the present tense because what happened on that morning is still happening to us and to the thousands whose loved ones did not come home that evening.

One hundred days later, that sacred ground's vigil light fire has been struck and we assess this Mystery of loss that has taken the seat next to us on our journey as a spectral figure might on our bus or plane. What has this companion of Mystery taken, what are we finding that we did not know we possessed, what are we learning that we did not know before?

We have lost our innocence, some tell us. What innocence, we ask, and did we ever have but half of it? Others say it is our invulnerability. What invulnerability? wonder those who prompt disappointing loves out of bittersweet memory as old men recall their youth in the aches of bones once broken.

What we lost is something we never had, the notion that we can *choose* our moments and call forth our lives as Michelangelo did figures from marble. That this illusion was hardly doubted makes its ruffled wake of heartbreak more poignant.

We weep as the dead tell us of so many plans based on *individual choice*. One bereft man tells us that he and his girlfriend planned "to get married when the time came to have children." Many speak of postponements — more schooling, a family trip, time together in retirement (there would always be more time) — and we agreed until time and chance intersected to sweep all choices away.

Lost is the American Dream that *choice* is our *right* so that morality consists not in *what* we choose but in *that* we choose. How empty the slogans — "No Limits," "No Fear," "You Can Have It All" — urged by the popular culture on men and women whose profound inner goodness deserves better.

In this loss we find obscured blessings: our sense of limitations and our mortality. In short, our human condition, this incomplete state that puts us on familiar terms with sin, death, and mischance. These are the everyday evidence of the imperfection that is our escape route from time into the eternal. In myths as old as the race, it is always the place where we stumble and fall that we find the gold.

Were we perfect, we would have no need of the experiences that transform our lives together. If perfect, we could never be lonely, never feel hurt, never be disappointed, never need to risk ourselves in loving another person.

Nor would we long for love or find it by surprise, as we learn that so many of the dead, young and old, already had. Perfection would exempt us from making acts of faith in others and sharing hope with them. These were second nature to so many men and women who, in the face of death's choosing them that day, wanted only to tell others that they loved them.

Out of the pits of loss, our searchers have retrieved long-neglected human treasures. Character does make a difference, and nothing is as strong as truth. The precious metal of honor has been found right next to duty, sacrifice, and forgiveness.

What have we learned if not our common calling and our true voice? Why have we, of all created beings, been given words if not to speak on behalf of all creation that, St. Paul tells us, groans and cries in expectation of deliverance?

We are the senses of the galaxies, called to recognize their pain in our own and to feel it on behalf of all being. We stand together as the chorus of the universe, singing in our suffering of all suffering and its healing through love. Our vocation is to see that no one suffers alone, that no pain goes unnoticed, and none is without meaning. We are the medium through which the cosmos feels its heartbreak but also the mediators of its comfort and resurrection.

We have learned no small amount at this place where we stumbled together a season ago, thinking that we had lost so much but finding instead the gold of the simplest and most lasting of our glories.

The Eyes of 9/11

March 13, 2002. Beauty and truth, we have been told, are in the eye of the beholder. They really lie in the eyes of those beheld. As the eye resembles the deep waters shimmering with every element of life, so our eyes do with every mystery of being human.

We learned this anew as CBS TV, whose symbol is an eye, broadcast "9/11," a documentary that functioned as our eyes do, investing the program with our natural way of looking at every day. We scan broad stretches, peer for a moment here, then glide, blurring the commonplace, searching out some detail, somebody or something familiar, "look there," we say later as we show our choppy home video, so like our eyes in its sweeps and distractions and sudden focusing.

So the camera catches out of the corner of its eye, as we would, the spurt of blood-like flame as the first silver knife slits the uplifted throat of Trade

Tower One. We are drawn into the great Mystery of our times, unable, as we say, to believe what we see with our own eyes. "Cast a cold eye," Yeats wrote, "on life, on death," but now we have looked on life and death together and our glance can never be cold and we cannot, as Yeats urges his imagined horseman, "pass by."

How variously and mysteriously and to how many purposes do we speak of the "eye." Love, Joseph Campbell wrote, comes first through the eyes. Sailors speak of the "eye of the wind," the direction opposite to the way it is blowing. And of the "eye of the storm," the center of calm at the hurricane's heart.

How right that nets lowered into that morning should yield meanings born of the sea. In mythology, the waters always symbolize the unconscious, the rich, silent, powerful flood of our human experience, that great gallery where hang our human images and symbols, the family album of our souls.

That day's double murder stirred us to recognize what we hold in common so that we looked at each with fresh eyes and beheld the mystery of how alike, instead of how different, we are. That morning we entered the eye of our time as Alice did the looking glass. Our own eyes were opened by its mud and dust as the blind man's were in the Gospel and we became mystics together inside this Mystery, *our* Mystery, of love and loss.

If "thy eye be single," the scriptures say again, "your whole being will be filled with light." That morning we saw how filled with light are so many men and women. Now we see them everywhere, in the streets and on the subways, through windows and in airport lines — the people who died that day streaming about us filled with light.

Our surrogate eye enters the vast lobby of the first tower to be struck. It is, indeed, a vast eye itself, cracked yet filled with September light, empty as only a silent space can feel after the noisy throng has passed through it.

Huddled there are the firemen, looped with hose and weighed down with equipment, glancing upward as they learn that the elevators are not working. In their eyes, and in those of the captains and chiefs dispatching them, we read every aspect of the Mystery in which they, and we, will be immersed.

Beneath their helmets their eyes measure the hundred-story climb, giving off the firefly sparks of urgency, the darting lights of duty and bravery through which they see the people cut off on the heights above. They flash other messages, too, of their tenderness for those they love, their regard for each other, the eyes of true men not looking, at this terrible moment, for a way out but for a way in.

The eyes of the chiefs reveal more of the mystery as they bark orders into radios and phones with no response, professionals trying to find out what we know, that the building is dying and hundreds of the firemen climbing the stairs will go down with it. A woman in the tide streaming down later tells columnist Mike Barnicle how she dreams of their faces and their eyes, noble and set, as they headed toward the darkness and death above.

We see Fire Chaplain Father Mychal Judge whispering prayers near the chiefs, their eyes those of fathers anxious for the sons they have sent to sea, filled with a growing sense that they stand together in the eye of destiny's perfect storm.

The documentary "9/11" is a sacrament of the life that looked death in the eye and stared it down that day.

Build Anything, Ground Zero's Spirit Will Still Be There

May 8, 2002. 9/11, the great sacramental event of our time, does not preach in words that ride away on the wind but in hushed revelation that possesses us as gently as a sunset or the gurgled smile of an infant. We stand with the living and the dead at Ground Zero that now resembles, in its vastness, emptiness, and mystery, the hidden desert that Jesus entered for forty days, the sweet desert that showered manna on the questing Jews, and the harsh desert that echoed with John the Baptist's proclamation that one greater than he was to come.

The 9/11 site sings of its Mystery as softly as the spirit does as it shuffles the desert sands. Here, we have spent most of a year like novices in a new religious order born out of the pain of history itself. What have we seen and what have we heard?

That the secular city is filled with faith, that the greatest of its wonders is ordinary and human-sized, just big enough to be borne in the heart. And that religion is not, as Bible-abusing preachers urge, a function of the will in training for title bouts with temptation.

The ordinary saints of 9/11 reveal that religion, like love, belongs to the whole personality, turning us toward rather than away from other people in searching for God. Religion enters us gently through our imaginations rather than tensely by way of the will. Faith, like first love, enters through the eyes, possessing us and leaving us hungry for sacraments, the loaves and fishes, the vigil lights in lovers' eyes, the body embraced and embracing, water to cleanse and wine to warm, oil to heal and salt to savor, each as right as love is for the earth. "I don't know any place," Robert Frost says, "it's likely to go better."

These elements are the open secrets of 9/11, the things the dead carried with them that morning, tethered with us on the lifeline of spiritual Mystery that was no mystery to them. Moments of silence at the site are as filled as late-night radio traffic with their plainsong litanies of wonders whose simplicity and purity blind us with their revelation.

Revelation has its origin in words for unveiling. Life's mysteries are out in the open, unveiled in every true human exchange, as in the thousands shared with us on 9/11. Religion is found in the last words of the ordinary saints of 9/11, in the final impulses, deep enough to sum up whole lives, and the law and the prophets, too, biblical vessels poured out but never emptied, all these men and women longing to tell someone else one more time, "I love you...."

The city's great newspaper says of the cleanup, "It is nearly done," and tells of retired fire captain John Vigiano who "has kept vigil there...ever since his only children — a police detective and a firefighter — disappeared in a summer morning's roar."[15]

Captain Vigiano is our Everyperson, whose sacramental presence at the site cannot be missed. We read that "construction workers, police officers and firefighters have formed a protective cocoon around" him. After they shake his hand, "they are slow to let go, as though some of his grace might be transferred through touch." As it has now, to all of us.

The eternal lifts off the site as well. We feel it as construction worker Jack Mirto did when, after working his sixty-five-ton excavator there for weeks, he found that "time had lost its meaning, how Thursday could just as well be Tuesday," and how laid-off workers were anxious to get back to that zone of mystery, pleading, "Get me a day, get me a night...."

Whatever is built to replace the towers, these spiritual realizations that link love, work, death, and eternal life will always be in this place. New buildings will be vessels of mystical truth, made sacred not just by memory but by the energy of human love, the central mystery of all religion, so lavishly expended here on 9/11, that will charge the air here forever.

Notes

1. See Dexter Filkins, "As Thick as the Ash, Myths Are Swirling," *New York Times,* September 25, 2001.

2. Nicholas Wade,"Body of St. Luke Gains Credibility," *New York Times,* October 16, 2001, p. A9.

3. "Still Searching for the 'Black Boxes,'" *Wall Street Journal,* October 17, 2001, pp. B1, B4.

4. CNS report from Vatican City, in *Catholic Weekly* (Michigan), October 12, 2001, p. 1.

5. Bryan Carovillano, " 'Danny Boy' Ban at Funeral Masses Stirs Chorus of Protest," AP, *Chicago Tribune,* October 21, 2001, Metro, sec. 2, p. 8.

6. Joseph Campbell, *Thou Art That: Transforming Religious Metaphor,* ed. Eugene Kennedy (Novato, Calif.: New World Library, 2001), p. 24.

7. Don Barry and Kevin Flynn, "Firefighters in Angry Scuffle with Police at Trade Center," *New York Times,* November 3, 2001, p. 1.

8. Dorothy Rabinowitz, "Neutral in the Newsroom," *Wall Street Journal,* November 6, 2001, p. A26.

9. Stephen Larsen, *The Mythic Imagination* (New York: Bantam Books, 1990), p. 194.

10. *New York Times*, November 23, 2001, p. B9.

11. *New York Times,* December 12, 2001, p. B1.

12. Campbell, *Thou Art That,* p. 65.

13. Ibid., p. 3.

14. *New York Times,* January 6, 2002, p. 1.

15. Dan Barry, "Mournful Task Ending, Forever Unfinished," *New York Times,* May 3, 2002, p. 1.